Connect
Workbook

W0080559

1

Jack C. Richards
Carlos Barbisan
with **Chuck Sandy**
and **Dorothy E. Zemach**

CAMBRIDGE
UNIVERSITY PRESS

CAMBRIDGE UNIVERSITY PRESS
Cambridge, New York, Melbourne, Madrid, Cape Town, Singapore, São Paulo

Cambridge University Press
40 West 20th Street, New York, NY 10011–4211, USA
www.cambridge.org
Information on this title:www.cambridge.org/9780521594950

First published 2004
5th printing 2006

Printed in Hong Kong by Golden Cup Printing Co. Ltd.

ISBN-13 978-0-521-59498-1 Student's Book 1 (English)
ISBN-10 0-521-59498-7 Student's Book 1 (English)
ISBN-13 978-0-521-60074-3 Student's Book 1 (Portuguese)
ISBN-10 0-521-60074-X Student's Book 1 (Portuguese)
ISBN-13 978-0-521-59495-0 Workbook 1 (English)
ISBN-10 0-521-59495-2 Workbook 1 (English)
ISBN-13 978-0-521-60070-5 Workbook 1 (Portuguese)
ISBN-10 0-521-60070-7 Workbook 1 (Portuguese)
ISBN-13 978-0-521-59494-3 Teacher's Manual 1 (English)
ISBN-10 0-521-59494-4 Teacher's Manual 1 (English)
ISBN-13 978-0-521-59492-9 Teacher's Manual 1 (Portuguese)
ISBN-10 0-521-59492-8 Teacher's Manual 1 (Portuguese)
ISBN-13 978-0-521-59491-2 Class Audio Cassettes 1
ISBN-10 0-521-59491-X Class Audio Cassettes 1
ISBN-13 978-0-521-59488-2 Class CD 1
ISBN-10 0-521-59488-X Class CD 1

Book design, art direction, and layout services: Adventure House, NYC

Table of Contents

1 Number the sentences in the correct order.

_____ Nice to meet you, Ana.

_____ My name is Ana.

_1_ Hi. I'm Valerie. What's your name?

_____ Nice to meet you, too.

2 Choose the correct words to complete the conversation.

A Hello. My name is Koji.
What's (Is / What's) your name?

B Hi, Koji. _____ (I'm / My) Joanie.
Nice to meet you.

A Nice to meet _____ (you / your), too.

3 Introduce yourself to John. Complete the conversation.

Hi. My name is John. What's your name?

_____

Nice to meet you.

_____

Lesson 2 Hello.

1 Look at the pictures. Complete the conversations with the sentences in the box.

☐ Fine, thank you. ☐ Good morning. ☑ How are you today?
☐ Good evening. ☐ How about you? ☐ Not too good.

1. **A** Good afternoon, Suzy.
   B *How are you today?*
   A _____
   B Great!

2. **A** _____
   How are you?
   B Not bad, thanks.
   _____
   A Good.

3. **A** _____
   B Hello, Mr. Gomez. How are you?
   A _____

2 Choose the correct titles.

1. I'm _Miss_ (Miss / Mrs.) Clark.
   I'm single.

2. My name is _____ (Ms. / Miss) Montes.
   I'm married.

3. I'm _____ (Mrs. / Mr.) Gold.
   I'm married.

4. My name is _____ (Mrs. / Ms.) Kim.
   I'm single.

Mini-review

1 There are 10 words in the puzzle. Find and circle 8 more words.
Look in these directions (→, ↓, ↘).

☐ are ☐ hi ☐ meet ☐ nice ☐ thanks
☐ hello ☐ how ☐ my ☑ not ☑ your

B	X	R	M	I	P	V	A	Q
N	I	C	E	Y	O	U	R	A
U	B	H	E	L	L	O	E	H
M	E	L	T	H	A	N	K	S
A	H	I	U	O	E	O	A	J
Z	U	K	R	W	D	T	G	C

2 Complete the conversations with the words from part 1.

1. **A** Hi, I'm Matt. What's _____ name?

   B _____ name is Eva.

   A _____ to meet you, Eva.

   B Nice to _____ you, too.

2. **A** _____ , Miss Valdes.

   B _____ , Corey. How _____ you today?

   A _____ bad. _____ about you?

   B Great, _____ .

3 Unscramble the sentences.

1. doGo / ofrotnaen. *Good afternoon.* _____

2. oyrSr / m'I / teal. _____

3. Hwo / rea / oyu? _____

4. ahWt's / oryu / eanm? _____

5. neFi, / haktns. _____

6. doGo / vngeine. _____

Lesson 3 After school

1 Choose the correct words to complete the conversations.

1. **A** _Hi_ (Hi / Bye), Anita.

   B Hello, Eric. This _____ (is / are) Sue Ross.

   A Nice to _____ (see / meet) you, Sue.

2. **A** _____ (Good-bye / Hello), Tony.

   B See you _____ (late / later), Mr. Acosta.

3. **A** _____ (Good-bye / Good evening), Ms. Green. How are you?

   B Hello. I'm good, _____ (thank / thanks).

4. **A** Mandy, _____ (you / this) is Ms. Parker.

   Ms. Parker, _____ (you / this) is Mandy Morgan.

   B Nice to meet _____ (you / your), Ms. Parker.

   C Nice to meet you, _____ (you / too), Mandy.

2 Match the pictures to the conversations in part 1.

a.

b.

c.

d.

3 Write the correct responses.

1. Gisele, this is Pedro.

   _____

2. Nice to meet you.

   _____

3. How are you today?

   _____

4. See you tomorrow.

   _____

Lesson 4 Names

1 Look at the pictures. Complete the forms for the students.

ENGLISH CLUB

Leticia Webber

Kenji Sato

Don Jackson

Carmen Lopes

1.
First Name: *Leticia*
Last Name: *Webber*

2.
First Name:
Last Name:

3.
First Name:
Last Name:

4.
First Name:
Last Name:

2 Match the questions to the answers.

1. Hello. How are you today? _d_

2. What's your name? ____

3. How do you spell your first name? ____

4. And how do you spell your last name? ____

a. Leticia Webber.

b. L-E-T-I-C-I-A.

c. W-E-B-B-E-R.

d. Good, thanks.

3 Complete the conversation in part 2 with your own information.

A *Hello. How are you today?* _____

You _____

A *What's your name?* _____

You _____

A _____

You _____

A _____

You _____

Lesson 5 Connections

1 Match the sentences to the responses.

1. How •   • tomorrow! •   • My name is Liz.
2. What's your •   • meet you. •   • Fine, thanks.
3. How do you spell your •   • are you? •   • T-A-Y-L-O-R
4. Nice to •   • last name? •   • Good-bye.
5. See you •   • name? •   • Nice to meet you, too.

2 Unscramble the questions. Then answer the questions with your own information.

1. you / How / are ?

   How are you?

   Fine, thank you.

2. your / What's / nickname ?

   _____

   _____

3. spell / do / your / How / name / first / you ?

   _____

   _____

4. name / your / last / What's ?

   _____

   _____

3 Look at the picture. Complete the conversation.

Pedro   **Carla**   **Sue**

A Good morning. My name's Pedro.

B Hi, I'm Sue.

A How are you today?

B _____

A This is my friend, Carla.

B _____

C Nice to meet you, too.

Unit 2 Favorite People

1 Who are the people in Cindy's life? Write two sentences for each number.

1. This is my computer partner.
   His name is Ken.

   This is my computer partner, Ken.

   Ken is my computer partner.

2. This is my best friend.
   Her name is Lisa.

   _____

   _____

3. This is my math teacher.
   His name is Mr. Miller.

   _____

   _____

4. This is my classmate.
   Her name is Mary.

   _____

   _____

2 Complete the conversations with *What's his name?*, *What's her name?*, or *Who's this?*

1. A *Who's this?* _____

   B My classmate.

2. A _____

   B Her name is Kayley.

3. A _____

   B This is my friend, James.

4. A _____

   B His name is Mr. Hill.

5. A _____

   B My coach.

6. A _____

   B Her name is Ms. Smith.

Lesson 7 Favorite stars

1 Complete the chart with the words in the box.

☑ basketball coach   ☐ classmate   ☐ model   ☐ soccer player
☐ best friend   ☐ computer partner   ☐ singer   ☐ TV star
☐ cartoon character   ☐ English teacher

People at school	Stars
basketball coach	

2 Unscramble the words. Then match them to the pictures and write sentences.

1. oelmd

     model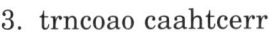

a. This is Madonna.

2. nsniet yrpale

b. This is Josh Hartnett.

3. trncoao caahtcerr

c. This is Serena Williams.

4. gnrsei

d. This is David Beckham.

5. troac

e. This is Tyson Beckford.
    He's my favorite model.

6. crceso eayplr

f. This is Snoopy.

Mini-review

1 Choose the correct response.

1.

   A What's her name?

   B *Her name is Kim.*

   ☐ I'm Lisa.

   ☑ Her name is Kim.

2.

   A Who's this?

   B _____

   ☐ His English teacher is Mrs. Mitchell.

   ☐ My best friend.

3.

   A Who's your favorite actor?

   B _____

   ☐ Russell Crowe.

   ☐ He's my classmate.

4.

   A What's his name?

   B _____

   ☐ His name is Mark.

   ☐ He's my tennis partner.

2 Unscramble the questions. Then answer the questions with your own information.

1. star / favorite / TV / your / Who's ?

   Q: *Who's your favorite TV star?*

   A: _____

2. name / What's / last / your ?

   Q: _____

   A: _____

3. teacher / your / Who's / English ?

   Q: _____

   A: _____

4. Who's / friend / best / your ?

   Q: _____

   A: _____

3 Complete the chart. Then write sentences about your favorites.

Star	Name	
1. model	*Naomi Campbell*	*She's my favorite model.*
2. singer	_____	_____
3. TV star	_____	_____
4. actor	_____	_____
5. cartoon character	_____	_____

Lesson 8 Birthday party

1 Write the numbers.

1. 7 _____seven_____
2. 18 _____
3. 20 _____
4. 6 _____

5. 12 _____
6. 3 _____
7. 19 _____
8. 11 _____

9. 4 _____
10. 16 _____
11. 8 _____
12. 1 _____

2 Circle the correct words to complete the conversation.

A Hi. My name's Carlos.

B (Good night / Hello). My name's John.

A (How / What) old (is / are) you?

B (You're / I'm) thirteen.

A (Who / How) about (your / my) little sister? (Is / Are) she six?

B (She's / He's) not (five / six). (She's / He's) four.

3 Write questions. Use the information in the chart.

	Louisa	Jeff	Keiko	Pedro
11	☑	☐	☐	☐
12	☐	☐	☐	☑
13	☐	☐	☑	☐
14	☐	☑	☐	☐

1. _How old is Jeff?_
   He's fourteen.

2. _____
   She's eleven.

3. _____
   He's twelve.

4. _____
   She's thirteen.

4 Correct the sentences. Use the information in the chart in part 3.

1. Pedro is eleven.
   Pedro is twelve.

2. Jeff is twelve.
   _____

3. Louisa is seventeen.
   _____

4. Keiko is ten.
   _____

Lesson 9 E-pals

1 Unscramble the questions. Then match the questions to the answers.

1. ehWre / ear / uoy / rmof? _b_

   Where are you from?

   a. She's not from Peru. She's from Colombia.

2. eehr'sW / nJho / omfr? ___

   b. I'm from Mexico.

3. rMai'sa / mfor / euPr, / grtih? ___

   c. I'm not from Japan. I'm from China.

4. 'ruYoe / fmro / pnaaJ, / hrgit? ___

   d. He's from France.

5. hWre'se / ehs / mrfo? ___

   e. He's not from Portugal. He's from Canada.

6. eH's / mofr / otgPuarl, / gtirh? ___

   f. She's from the U.S.

2 Write questions and answers.

1. she? / Australia

   A _Where's she from?_

   B _She's from Australia._

2. he? / Colombia

   A ___

   B ___

3. she from Mexico, right? / from Brazil

   A ___

   B ___

4. he from Germany, right? / from the U.S.

   A ___

   B ___

5. you? / Brazil

   A ___

   B ___

6. she? / Venezuela

   A ___

   B ___

12   Unit 2

Connections

1 Write questions.

1. **A** *How old are you?*
   B I'm thirteen.

2. **A** _____
   B I'm from Brazil.

3. **A** _____
   B This is my best friend.

4. **A** _____
   B His name is Tony.

5. **A** _____
   B My favorite soccer player is
   Roberto Carlos.

6. **A** _____
   B My favorite actor is Kate Hudson.

2 Complete the questions with *Who's*, *Where*, or *How*. Then answer
the questions with your own information.

1. *Who's* your best friend?

   _____

2. _____ old are you?

   _____

3. _____ are you from?

   _____

4. _____ your favorite singer?

   _____

⑪ What a mess!

1 Unscramble the words. Check (✓) the things that you have with you.

☑ 1. s r r e a e   *eraser*

☐ 2. e a a m c r   _____

☐ 3. k t b o e o o n   _____

☐ 4. s b r h u   _____

☐ 5. n e p   _____

☐ 6. l u b a m r l e   _____

☐ 7. a k a k b c p c   _____

☐ 8. a t h   _____

2 Write sentences with *This is* or *That's*.

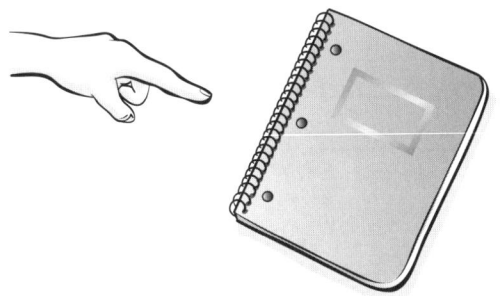

1. (Amy) *This is Amy's backpack.*

2. (Nick) _____

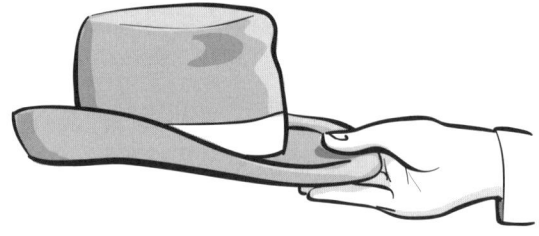

3. (Ricardo) _____

4. (John) _____

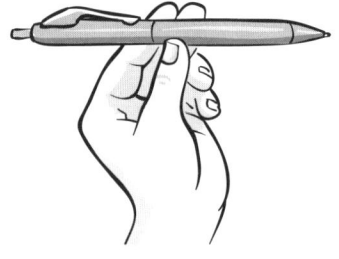

5. (Brad) _____

6. (Erica) _____

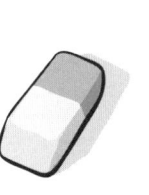

7. (Ken) _____

8. (Viviana) _____

Cool things

1 Write questions. Then write *a* or *an* to complete the answers.

1. *What's that?*

   It's __a__ video game.

2. _____

   It's _____ alarm clock.

3. _____

   It's _____ radio.

4. _____

   It's _____ cell phone.

5. _____

   It's _____ electronic organizer.

6. _____

   It's _____ umbrella.

2 Number the sentences in the correct order.

____ Wow! It's really cool!

____ No, it's not. It's a television.

____ Hmm. It's weird. And what's that?

____ It's a radio.

_1_ Maria, what's this? A computer?

1 What does Stacy say about her things? Write sentences.

1. *That's my cell phone.*
2. _____
3. _____
4. _____

5. _____
6. _____
7. _____
8. _____

2 Circle the correct words to complete the conversation.

Man Good morning. This is your bag, right?

Stacy Yes. This is (my / your) bag.

Man (Who's / What's) this?

Stacy It's (a / an) alarm clock.

Man An alarm clock? Really?

Stacy Yes. It's (a / an) radio, too.

Man I see. What's (it / that)?

Stacy Oh, it's (a / an) electronic organizer.

3 Check (✓) the correct response.

1. What's this?
   - ☑ It's a notebook.
   - ☐ Hmm. It's weird.

2. What's that? A cell phone?
   - ☐ Really? It's great!
   - ☐ No, it's not. It's an address book.

3. And what's that?
   - ☐ That's Christina's pen.
   - ☐ Wow! It's really cool.

4. Hey, Carlos. What's this?
   - ☐ What's that? A computer?
   - ☐ It's Molly's computer.

13 Favorite things

1 **Complete the words.**

1. c _o_ m i c _b_ o _o_ k   2. __ - s __ __ __ t   3. __ __ s __ e __ __

4. __ i __ __ l e   5. __ r __ d __ __ __ c __ __ __ s   6. __ __ t __ h __ __

2 **Unscramble the sentences to make a conversation.**

A these, / Chris / are / What ?
What are these, Chris?

B cards / my / They're / trading / favorite .
_____

A They're cool. / are / What / those ?
_____

B my / They're / T-shirts .
_____

A They're . . . nice.

3 **Complete the conversations with the sentences in the box.**

☐ Hmm. They're very interesting.   ☑ Those are my favorite comic books.
☐ These are my posters.   ☐ What are these?

1. **A** What are those?

   B _Those are my favorite comic books._

2. **A** _____

   B They're my trading cards.

3. **A** Those are my favorite video games.

   B _____

4. **A** _____

   B Oh, they're nice.

Where is it?

1 Look at the picture. Write questions and answers.

1. **Q:** _Where's the umbrella?_

   A: It's next to the dresser.

2. **Q:** _____

   A: They're on the bed.

3. **Q:** _____

   A: It's in the wastebasket.

4. **Q:** Where are the T-shirts?

   A: _____

5. **Q:** Where's the bag?

   A: _____

6. **Q:** Where are the comic books?

   A: _____

2 Choose the correct words to complete the conversation.

Billy Mom! I'm late. _Where's_ (Where's / Where are)
my soccer ball?

Mom _____ (It's / They're) under
your bed.

Billy OK, but _____ (where's / where are)
my books? _____ (It's not / They're not)
on my desk.

Mom _____ (It's / They're) on your dresser.

Billy Oh, right. Thanks.
And _____ (where's / where are)
my calculator? _____ (It's not / They're not)
in my bag.

Mom _____ (It's / They're) under
your desk.

15 Connections

1 Look at the picture and answer the questions.

1. What's her name?

   Her name is Elizabeth.

2. Where's she from?

   _____

3. How old is she? Fifteen?

   _____

4. What's her nickname?

   _____

Elizabeth Benson
(Lizzy)
Age 13
🍁 Canada

2 Look at the picture and write the questions.

Miguel Rios
Age 12
Mexico

1. *What's his first name?*

   Miguel.

2. _____

   He's from Mexico.

3. _____

   They're his comic books.

4. _____

   He's twelve years old.

3 Match the questions to the answers.

1. Where's my hat? _d_
2. What's this? ____
3. Where are my comic books? ____
4. What are these? ____
5. What's that? ____
6. What are those? ____

a. It's an electronic organizer.
b. They're Mike's video games.
c. They're in your room.
d. It's under your bag.
e. Those are trading cards.
f. That's my notebook.

Lesson 16 At the movies

1 Look at the picture. Are the statements true or false?
Check (✓) True or False.

		True	False			True	False
1.	Linda is at the movie theater.	✓	☐	4. Greg is at the bank.		☐	☐
2.	Paul is at the shoe store.	☐	☐	5. Dave is at the shoe store.		☐	☐
3.	Aya is at the subway station.	☐	☐	6. Jane is at the Internet café.		☐	☐

2 Unscramble the sentences.

1. **A** you / the / newsstand / Are / near ?

   Are you near the newsstand?

   B not. / No, / I'm / the / at / I'm / movie theater .

   _____

2. **A** still / Are / the / Internet café / you / at ?

   _____

   B I'm / No, / not. / bus stop / at / I'm / the .

   _____

3 Complete the conversations.

1. **A** *Are you twelve?* (twelve)

   B No, I'm not. I'm eleven.

2. **A** _____ (Mexico City)

   B No, I'm not. I'm from Barcelona.

3. **A** _____ (soccer player)

   B Yes, I am. It's my favorite sport.

4. **A** _____ (Salma Hayek fan)

   B Yes, I am. She's my favorite star.

Lesson 17 Downtown

1 Look at the picture. Write sentences with the words in the box.

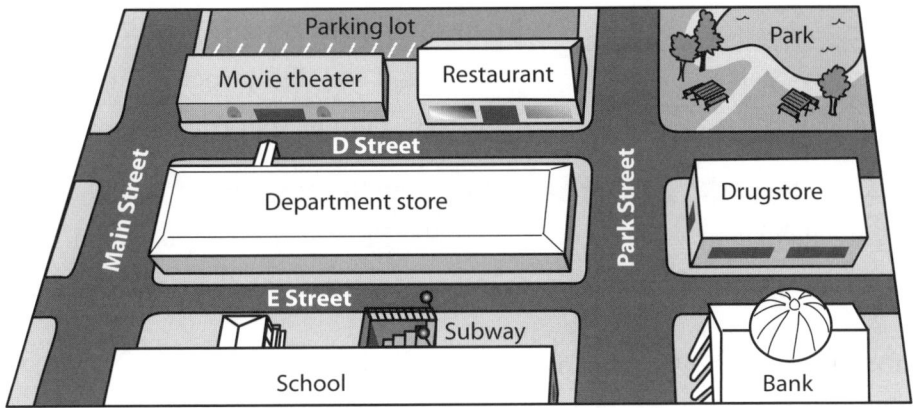

1. (movie theater / restaurant)

   The movie theater is next to the restaurant.

2. (parking lot / movie theater and restaurant)

   _____

3. (department store / D Street)

   _____

4. (subway station / school)

   _____

5. (drugstore / park / bank)

   _____

☐ behind
☐ between
☐ in front of
☑ next to
☐ on

2 Look at the picture in part 1. Answer the questions. If the answer is *no*, give the correct information.

1. Is the movie theater on E Street?

   No, it's not. It's on D Street.

2. Is the department store next to the movie theater?

   _____

3. Is the movie theater across from the department store?

   _____

4. Is the restaurant next to the department store?

   _____

5. Is the parking lot in front of the movie theater?

   _____

Mini-review

1 Check (✓) the correct response.

1. Are you at home?
   - ✓ Yes, I am. I'm in my room.
   - ☐ Yes, it is. It's on Oak Street.

2. Is your school next to the park?
   - ☐ Yes, I am. I'm at school.
   - ☐ No, it isn't. It's across from the park.

3. Are you from Brazil?
   - ☐ Yes, I am. I'm a soccer fan.
   - ☐ No, I'm not. I'm from Peru.

4. Are you 13 years old?
   - ☐ No, I'm not. I'm 14 years old.
   - ☐ Yes, I'm still at the basketball game.

2 Answer the questions in part 1 with your own information.

1. _____
2. _____
3. _____
4. _____

3 Look at the picture. Then circle the correct words to complete the sentences.

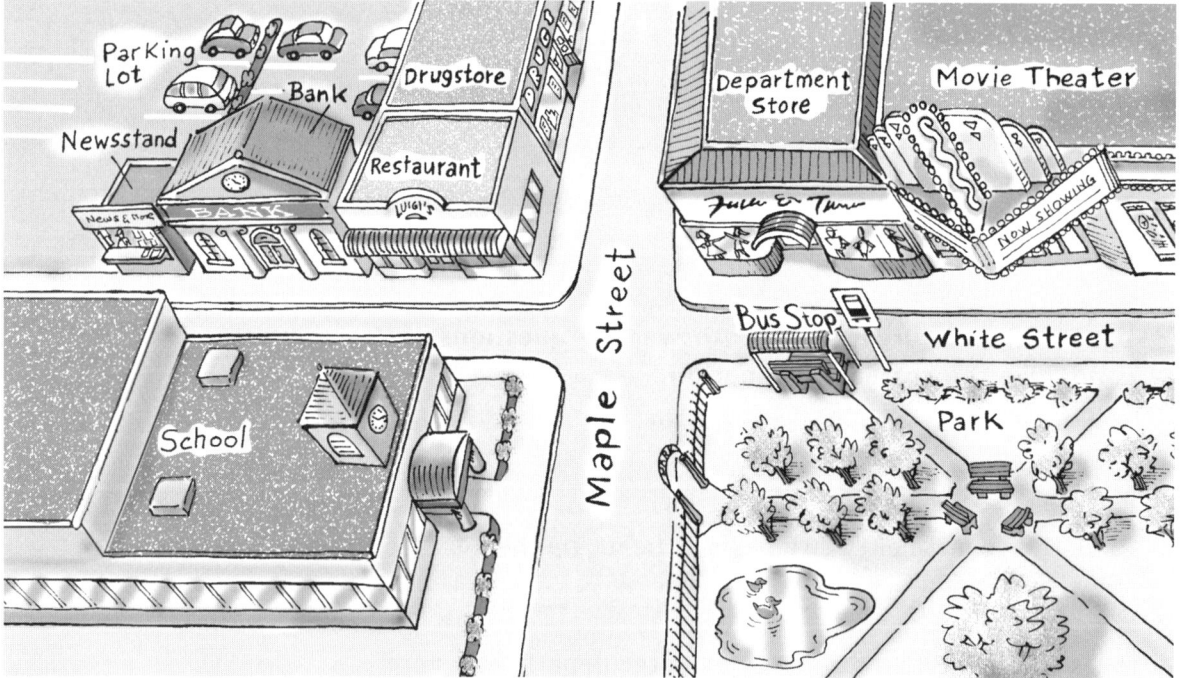

1. The bank is (between / in front of) the newsstand and the restaurant.

2. The drugstore is (behind / on) Maple Street.

3. The bus stop is (across from / in front of) the department store.

4. The movie theater is (next to / between) the department store.

5. The parking lot is (on / behind) the bank.

6. The school is (across from / next to) the park.

Lesson

18 At the mall

1 Unscramble and write the words. Then match the words to make the names of places.

1. s u b   _____bus_____ •   • store

2. l o g b i w n   _____ •   • arcade

3. n g k a s t i   _____ •   • theater

4. v e i m o   _____ •   • lot

5. r n a i k p g   _____ •   • stop

6. i o e d v   _____ •   • rink

7. a y c n d   _____ •   • alley

2 Write questions and answers.

Hitomi / bus stop

Q: *Is Hitomi at the bus stop?*

A: *No, she's not. She's at the skating rink.*

Eric and Kelly / Internet café

Q: _____

A: _____

Kevin / candy store

Q: _____

A: _____

Emily and Maria / video arcade

Q: _____

A: _____

Julia / skating rink

Q: _____

A: _____

Pedro / bookstore

Q: _____

A: _____

19 Any suggestions?

1 Look at the picture. Write sentences using *bored, hot, hungry, thirsty,* or *tired.* Then match each sentence to the correct suggestion.

1. Kevin   *I'm bored.*   •   • Go swimming.

2. Cindy   _____ •   • Have a soda.

3. Donna   _____ •   • Sit down.

4. Kyle   _____ •   • Have a sandwich.

5. Amy   _____ •   • Play volleyball.

2 Number the sentences in the correct order.

_____ Bored? Well, go swimming or play volleyball.

_1_ Hello, Karen. How are you?

_____ But I'm tired, too. I'm tired and bored.

_____ Oh, hi, Jim. I'm bored.

_____ OK. Go to a movie. There's a good movie at the new movie theater.

_____ Good idea. Let's go together.

3 How do you feel? Write sentences with *I'm* or *I'm not.* Use your own information.

1. (bored)   _____

2. (hungry)   _____

3. (tired)   _____

4. (hot)   _____

5. (thirsty)   _____

Lesson 20 Connections

1 Complete the conversations with the phrases and sentences in the box.

☐ Are they   ☐ No, he's not.   ☐ Yes, he is.
☐ Are you   ☐ No, I'm not.   ☐ Yes, I am.
☑ Is he   ☐ No, they're not.   ☐ Yes, they are.

1. **A** Where's Takua? ___*Is he*___ at the bookstore?

   B _____ . He's at the café.

   A Oh. Is he hungry?

   B _____ . And he's thirsty, too.

2. **A** Excuse me. _____ Mrs. Hills?

   B _____ . I'm Ms. Silva.

   A Oh! I'm sorry. Are you a teacher?

   B _____ . I'm your English teacher!

3. **A** Are Alex and Steve still at the park?

   B _____ . They're at the bus stop.

   A Oh. _____ tired?

   B _____ .

2 Complete the sentences with *go, have, play,* or *sit.*

1. ___*Play*___ soccer in the park.
2. _____ swimming at the beach.
3. _____ down and play video games.
4. _____ a sandwich at a restaurant.
5. _____ to a store.
6. _____ a soda at a café.
7. _____ down on the bus.
8. _____ volleyball at school.

3 Circle the correct words to complete the sentences.

1. I'm really bored. Let's (have / ⟨play⟩) tennis.
2. I'm hot. Let's (go / play) swimming at the beach.
3. I'm bored. Let's (have / go) to the video arcade.
4. I'm tired. Let's (go / sit) down.
5. I'm hungry. Let's (go / play) to a café.
6. I'm thirsty. Let's (sit / have) a soda.

21 My family

1 Look at the picture. Complete the sentences.

George, 65   Betty, 63

Eric, 44   Lauren, 42   Gary, 32   Nancy, 30

Justin, 10   Kate, 12   Ellen, 8   Kelly, 2

1. Justin is Kate's _____brother_____ . He's _10_ .
2. Gary is Kate's _____ . He's _____ .
3. Betty is Kate's _____ . She's _____ .
4. Eric is Kate's _____ . He's _____ .
5. Ellen is Kate's _____ . She's _____ .
6. Lauren is Kate's _____ . She's _____ .
7. Kelly is Kate's _____ . She's _____ .
8. Nancy is Kate's _____ . She's _____ .
9. George is Kate's _____ . He's _____ .

2 Write sentences about Kate's family. Use *have* or *has*.

1. Kate's parents / three children

   Kate's parents have three children.

2. Justin / two sisters

   _____

3. Kate, Justin, and Ellen / one cousin

   _____

4. Lauren / one brother

   _____

5. Kate / one aunt and one uncle

   _____

6. Justin / brothers

   _____

7. Ellen / aunt

   _____

8. Gary / sister

   _____

9. Kate / one sister and one brother

   _____

10. Kelly / sisters or brothers

    _____

Lesson 22 Family reunion

1 There are 10 words in the puzzle. Find and circle 8 more words.
Look across (→) and down (↓).

☐ crazy   ☐ funny   ☑ pretty   ☑ shy   ☐ tall
☐ friendly   ☐ handsome   ☐ short   ☐ smart   ☐ thin

S	P	F	U	N	N	Y	L	X	Y	R	H
M	G	L	W	A	I	P	P	Y	B	D	A
A	O	Z	S	H	O	R	T	R	F	L	N
R	B	S	F	R	I	E	N	D	L	Y	D
T	H	I	N	U	K	T	C	P	A	E	S
L	J	M	C	D	A	T	T	R	V	P	O
I	K	W	O	S	H	Y	G	B	H	Z	M
T	A	L	L	X	C	R	A	Z	Y	B	E

2 Number the sentences in the correct order.

_____ Kayla? She's friendly and very funny.

_____ He's smart. He's shy, too.

_1_ What's his name?

_____ And your sister? What's she like?

_____ His name is Mike. He's my brother.

_____ What's he like?

_____ Well, you're friendly and funny, too!

3 Answer the questions with your own information.

1. What's your best friend like?

_____

2. What's your favorite actor like?

_____

3. What's your math teacher like?

_____

4. What are you like?

_____

Mini-review

1 Check (✓) the word that is different.

1. ☐ thirty	☐ twenty-three	☑ friendly	☐ sixty
2. ☐ uncle	☐ brother	☐ sister	☐ friend
3. ☐ hungry	☐ handsome	☐ tall	☐ thin
4. ☐ friendly	☐ funny	☐ smart	☐ seventy
5. ☐ mother	☐ father	☐ teacher	☐ aunt

2 Unscramble the sentences.

Leonardo

1. a / small / family / very / has / Leonardo
   Leonardo has a very small family.

2. brother / has / He / a
   _____

3. His / tall / is / brother
   _____

4. no / has / Leonardo / sisters
   _____

5. mother / two / sisters / His / has
   _____

6. is / only / His / an / child / father
   _____

3 Laura is talking to Nick. Complete her sentences with *have*, *has*, or *'s*.

My name _'s_ Laura. I ____ one brother. He ____ eight, and his name ____ Vincent. He ____ really funny. I ____ a best friend. Her name ____ Julie. Julie ____ a little sister. She ____ only three. Her name ____ Kristen, and she ____ very pretty. Julie ____ a brother, too. He ____ handsome.

Lesson 23 My new city

1 Match the words to the correct pictures.

1. happy _c_
2. old ____
3. sad ____
4. new ____
5. big ____
6. quiet ____

2 Complete the sentences with the words in part 1.

1. Their neighborhood is noisy. It's not ___quiet___ .
2. Their school is old. It's not _____ .
3. We're sad. We're not _____ .
4. Our house is small. It's not _____ .

3 Combine the sentences. Use *they're*, *we're*, *their*, or *our*.

1. You're happy. I'm happy, too.
   We're happy.

2. Her neighborhood is quiet. His neighborhood is quiet, too.
   _____

3. He's from Canada. She's from Canada, too.
   _____

4. I'm a little sad. You're a little sad, too.
   _____

5. My school is new. Your school is new, too.
   _____

4 Circle the correct words to complete the sentences.

1. (They're / Their) school is very nice.
2. We miss Taro, but (our / we're) happy for him.
3. (They're / Our) soccer team is great this year.
4. (Their / We're) last name is Robbins.
5. (They're / Their) from Brazil.
6. (They're / Our) friends are funny.
7. (They're / Their) house isn't big.
8. (We're / Our) teacher is nice.
9. (They're / Their) not from Mexico.
10. (We're / Our) not thirsty.

 24 At home

1 Match the words in the box to the rooms in the house. Write the numbers.

❶ bathroom ❸ dining room ❺ kitchen ❼ yard
❷ bedroom ❹ garage ❻ living room

2 Complete the paragraph about the house in part 1.
Use *it's* or *it has.*

This is a new house. __It's__ big. _____ in the city, so _____ a small yard.
_____ four bedrooms and two bathrooms. _____ a nice kitchen and a big
dining room. _____ a living room, too. _____ small, but pretty. _____ a garage.
The neighborhood is nice. _____ quiet.

3 Circle the words that make the sentences true for you.

1. My home is in the (city / country).

2. It's (old / new).

3. Our neighborhood is (quiet / noisy).

4. Our (house / apartment) has a (big / small) kitchen.

5. It has (one / two / three / four / five) bedrooms.

25 Connections

1 Complete the paragraphs about Bianca with the words in the box.

| ☑ has | ☐ have | ☐ It has | ☐ It's | ☐ Our | ☐ Their | ☐ They're | ☐ We're |

   This is my best friend, Bianca. She is 14 years old. She __*has*__ one brother and one sister. _____ really friendly. She has a dog. It's cute.

   Bianca and I are in the same math class. _____ also on the same soccer team. _____ team is pretty good. We _____ two coaches. _____ names are Mr. Suarez and Mr. Cooper.

   Bianca lives in a big house. _____ in the country. _____ a big yard.

2 Match the questions to the answers.

1. What's your bedroom like? __*d*__   a. They're smart and funny.

2. Where is your home? ____   b. It's big and noisy. It has great teachers.

3. What's unusual about your home? ____   c. It's in the country.

4. What are your friends like? ____   d. It's small and quiet.

5. What's your school like? ____   e. It has six bathrooms.

6. What's your mother like? ____   f. She's really friendly.

3 Answer the questions in part 2 with your own information.

1. _____

2. _____

3. _____

4. _____

5. _____

6. _____

Lesson 26 The Media Center

1 Complete the crossword puzzle.

Across

Down

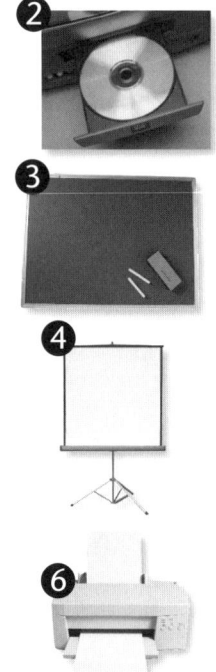

2 Complete the sentences with *there's a*, *there's no*, *there are*, or *there are no*.

1. _There are_ two printers.   5. _____ three cassette players.

2. _____ bookcase.   6. _____ CD player.

3. _____ board.   7. _____ VCR.

4. _____ screens.   8. _____ cabinets.

Lesson 27 Around school

1 Complete the chart with the words in the box.

☐ auditorium ☐ cafeteria ☐ football field ☐ language lab ☐ swimming pool
☑ baseball field ☐ computer lab ☐ gym ☐ library ☐ tennis court

Sports facilities	School facilities
baseball field	

2 Circle the correct words to complete the conversation.

Angelo Rey, your school is cool. (Is / Are) there a gym?

Rey Yes, there (is / are). There (is / are) three athletic fields, too.

Angelo (Are / Is) there (a / any) good football players?

Rey No, there (are / aren't). There (is / are) some good baseball players.

Angelo Is there (a / any) swimming pool?

Rey No, there (is / isn't). But there is a cafeteria. It's great!

Angelo Good. I'm hungry. Let's have a sandwich!

3 Complete the questions with *Is there a* or *Are there any*. Then answer the questions with your own information.

1. _Is there a_____ swimming pool at your house?

   _____

2. _____ media center at your school?

   _____

3. _____ athletic fields in your neighborhood?

   _____

4. _____ tennis courts on your street?

   _____

5. _____ cafeteria at your school?

   _____

At School 33

1 Unscramble and write the words. Then match the words to make the names of places and things.

1. d i o v e   _video_ •   • lab

2. u p c t m o r e   _____ •   • cassette recorder

3. n e t n i s   _____ •   • field

4. c l e t h a i t   _____ •   • center

5. t a s e c e t s   _____ •   • player

6. g w i s n m i m   _____ •   • pool

7. i a e d m   _____ •   • court

2 Complete the conversations.

1. **A** Are the facilities in your school nice? (Yes)

   B _Yes, they are._ We have great facilities!

2. **A** Are there any tennis courts at your school? (No)

   B _____ But we have three soccer fields.

3. **A** Is the gym in your school next to the cafeteria? (No)

   B _____ It's next to the library.

4. **A** Are there any new students in your class? (Yes)

   B _____ They're from Puerto Rico.

5. **A** Is there a media center in your school? (Yes)

   B _____ It's new and big.

6. **A** Are there any good soccer players in your school? (Yes)

   B _____ Their names are Emily and Hugo.

7. **A** Is there a VCR in your classroom? (No)

   B _____ But there's a VCR in the media center.

8. **A** Is there a park near your school? (Yes)

   B _____ It's on Oak Street.

3 Answer the questions in part 2 with your own information.

1. _____   5. _____

2. _____   6. _____

3. _____   7. _____

4. _____   8. _____

28 School subjects

1 Complete the words.

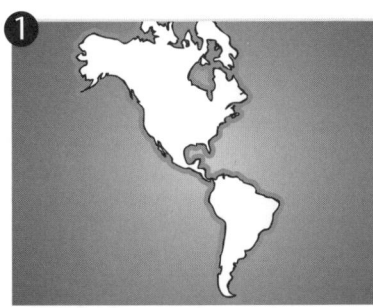

g e o g r a p h y

_ i _ _ _ _ y

_ _ _ h

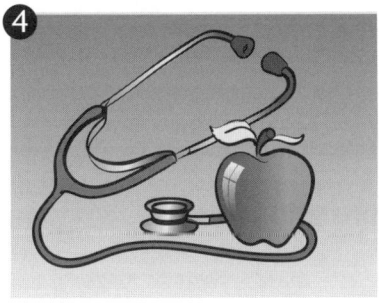

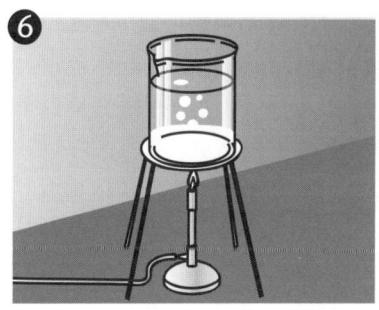

_ _ _ l _ h

_ u _ _ _

_ c _ _ _ c _

2 Complete the paragraph with *on* or *at*.

My school schedule is crazy! I have science ___at___ 8:30 _____ Monday, Wednesday, and Friday. I think science is easy. I have math _____ 10:00 every day. Math is difficult. I have music _____ Tuesday and Thursday _____ 11:00. It's fun. I have computer lab _____ Monday and Wednesday _____ 1:00. It's my favorite class. I don't like history. I have history every day _____ 2:00.

3 Are these statements true or false for you? Write *T* (true) or *F* (false). Then correct the false statements.

1. I have six classes every day. _____

_____

2. History is my favorite class. _____

_____

3. I have English on Monday. _____

_____

4. Art is difficult. _____

_____

5. I think science is easy. _____

_____

6. I have math at 10:45 on Monday. _____

_____

Lesson 29 Spring Day

1 Write the times another way.

1. It's eight forty-five.

   It's a quarter to nine.

2. It's two fifty.

   _____

3. It's seven fifteen.

   _____

4. It's three twenty-five.

   _____

5. It's twelve forty.

   _____

6. It's eleven fifty-five.

   _____

2 What time is it now? Write the answer two ways.

_____

_____

3 Look at the information on Jake's schedule. Write questions and answers.

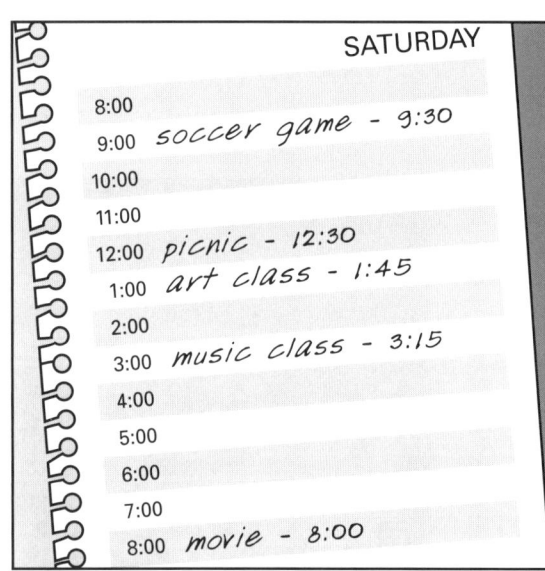

SATURDAY

8:00
9:00 soccer game - 9:30
10:00
11:00
12:00 picnic - 12:30
1:00 art class - 1:45
2:00
3:00 music class - 3:15
4:00
5:00
6:00
7:00
8:00 movie - 8:00

1. **Q:** _What time is the soccer game?_

   A: It's at nine thirty.

2. **Q:** What time is the movie?

   A: _____

3. **Q:** _____

   A: It's at three fifteen.

4. **Q:** What time is the picnic?

   A: _____

5. **Q:** What time is his art class?

   A: _____

4 What time is it now? Write the times.

1.

   It's eleven o'clock.

2.

   _____

3.

   _____

4.

   _____

5.

   _____

6.

   _____

Lesson 30 Connections

1 Check (✓) the word that is different.

1. ☐ auditorium   ☑ soccer field   ☐ library   ☐ computer lab
2. ☐ screen   ☐ history   ☐ health   ☐ geography
3. ☐ CD player   ☐ bookcase   ☐ printer   ☐ picnic
4. ☐ math   ☐ science   ☐ spelling contest   ☐ English
5. ☐ gym   ☐ Spanish   ☐ swimming pool   ☐ tennis court
6. ☐ VCR   ☐ bicycle race   ☐ band concert   ☐ fashion show

2 Complete the conversations with the questions in the box.

> ☐ Are there any cassette players in the media center?
> ☐ Is there a baseball game today?
> ☑ What is your favorite class in school?
> ☐ What time is the spelling contest?
> ☐ When is your Spanish class?

1. **A** _What is your favorite class in school?_
   B My favorite class is computer class.

2. **A** _____
   B Yes, there is. It's at seven fifteen.

3. **A** _____
   B No, there aren't. But there are some CD players.

4. **A** _____
   B The spelling contest? It's at three o'clock.

5. **A** _____
   B It's on Wednesday at nine forty-five.

3 Complete the chart with the words in the box.

> ☐ auditorium   ☑ geography   ☐ language lab   ☐ math   ☐ science
> ☐ CD player   ☐ history   ☐ library   ☐ printer   ☐ screen

Subjects	Facilities	Equipment
geography	_____	_____
_____	_____	_____
_____	_____	_____
_____	_____	_____

1 There are 8 countries in the puzzle. Find and circle 7 more countries. Look in these directions (→ , ↓ , ↘).

☑ Belize ☐ England ☐ New Zealand ☐ South Africa
☐ Canada ☐ India ☐ Singapore ☐ the United States

T	H	E	U	N	I	T	E	D	S	T	A	T	E	S
P	S	S	Y	R	A	Q	W	N	B	I	M	Z	V	I
C	X	D	M	S	U	I	S	M	G	I	R	Y	W	N
A	P	X	G	C	R	P	W	Y	V	L	D	A	C	G
N	B	Z	Y	T	P	U	N	X	W	I	A	N	E	A
A	Q	U	K	A	K	T	R	I	V	N	Q	N	O	P
D	N	E	W	Z	E	A	L	A	N	D	U	W	D	O
A	B	A	Z	P	K	R	M	O	X	I	M	Y	E	R
O	L	K	E	Y	C	M	N	P	O	A	Z	I	W	E
T	S	O	U	T	H	A	F	R	I	C	A	R	U	B
L	A	B	E	L	I	Z	E	R	I	G	O	G	W	I

2 Circle the correct words to complete the conversation.

Carla You have a lot of friends, José. Are they from Belize?

José No, they (are / aren't). They're from England.

Carla And this girl? (Is / Are) she from England?

José Yes, she (is / isn't). She's great.

Carla This boy is cute. (Is / Are) he from England, too?

José No, he (aren't / isn't). (He's / She's) from Canada. He has six sisters.

Carla Wow!

3 Complete the questions with *is* or *are*. Then answer the questions with your own information.

1. _____ your city or town in the U.S.? _____

2. _____ you from South Africa? _____

3. _____ your teachers from England? _____

4. _____ your best friend from India? _____

Lesson 32 Nationalities

1 Write the sentences another way.

1. Patricia is from Brazil.

   She's Brazilian.

3. Mick and Bruce are from Australia.

   _____

5. Peter is from England.

   _____

2. Alma is from Puerto Rico.

   _____

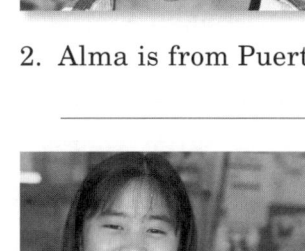

4. Naoko is from Japan.

   _____

6. Josh and Jill are from the United States.

   _____

2 Are these statements true or false for you? Check (✓) True or False.
Then correct the false statements.

	True	False
1. My first language is English.	☐	☑

   My first language isn't English. It's Spanish.

| 2. My parents are from Spain. | ☐ | ☐ |

   _____

| 3. My English teacher is Canadian. | ☐ | ☐ |

   _____

| 4. My favorite cartoon character is Japanese. | ☐ | ☐ |

   _____

| 5. My favorite actor is from Mexico. | ☐ | ☐ |

   _____

| 6. My best friend is from Puerto Rico. | ☐ | ☐ |

   _____

Around the World   39

1 Check (✓) the word that is different.

1. ☐ American   ☐ Peruvian   ☐ French   ☑ Japan
2. ☐ Canada   ☐ England   ☐ Rio de Janeiro   ☐ Peru
3. ☐ Australia   ☐ Mexico   ☐ South Korean   ☐ Brazil
4. ☐ Japanese   ☐ Spain   ☐ Peruvian   ☐ Mexican
5. ☐ Brazilian   ☐ England   ☐ Canada   ☐ the United States

2 Complete the paragraph with *is*, *isn't*, *are*, and *aren't*.

My favorite actor ___*is*___ Jackie Chan. Jackie _____ from China. He _____ American, but he _____ a big star in the United States. Some of his movies _____ in Chinese. They _____ all in English. His movies _____ usually sad and quiet. They _____ funny and loud. He _____ tall, but he _____ cute.

3 Check (✓) the correct response.

1. Is he from Vancouver?
   - ☐ No, they aren't.
   - ☑ Yes, he is.

2. Is Russell Crowe Canadian?
   - ☐ Yes, it is.
   - ☐ No, he isn't. He's Australian.

3. Are they from France?
   - ☐ Yes, they are.
   - ☐ Yes, she is.

4. Is she from Japan?
   - ☐ No, he isn't. He's from South Korea.
   - ☐ Yes, she is. She's a famous singer.

5. Are Marco and Sergio from South Africa?
   - ☐ No, they aren't. They're from Brazil.
   - ☐ Yes, they are great baseball players.

6. Is Gil de Ferran Brazilian?
   - ☐ Yes, he is. He's great.
   - ☐ Yes, they are. They're interesting.

Lesson 33 Holidays

1 Unscramble and write the months.

1. moreeNvb _____
2. uaJrayn _____
3. acMhr _____
4. epmeeStbr _____

5. arerFbuy _____
6. uusAgt _____
7. rcboOte _____
8. ipAlr _____

2 Write the missing months.

1. September   October   *November*   _____
2. March   _____   May   _____
3. _____   February   _____   April
4. June   _____   August   _____
5. _____   March   April   _____
6. _____   _____   December   _____

3 Complete the conversations with the sentences in the box.

☐ It's in February.
☐ It's in May.
☐ It's in October. It's a fun holiday.
☐ It's July. My favorite holiday is Independence Day.
☐ It's New Year's Eve. It's in December.
☑ Yes, it is. It's great.

1. **A** Is Halloween your favorite holiday?
   B *Yes, it is. It's great.* _____

2. **A** When is Valentine's Day?
   B _____

3. **A** When is Thanksgiving in Canada?
   B _____

4. **A** When is Mother's Day?
   B _____

5. **A** What's your favorite holiday?
   B _____

6. **A** What's your favorite month?
   B _____

Important days

1 Complete the crossword puzzle with these words.

Across

  5. 18th

  6. 24th

  8. 1st

  9. 3rd

10. 30th

Down

  1. 6th

  2. 17th

  3. 10th

  4. 13th

  7. 5th

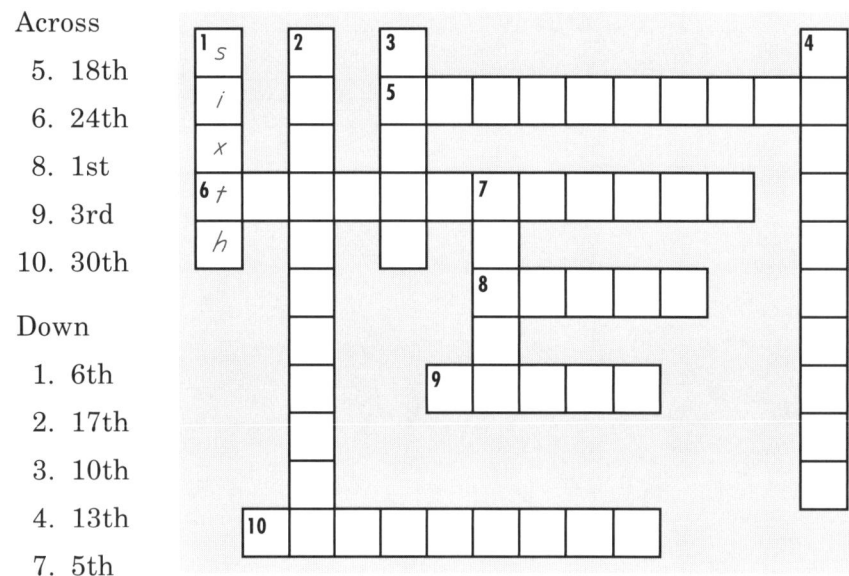

2 Complete the paragraph with *in* or *on*.

     Halloween is __on__ October 31st, Thanksgiving is _____ November, and Christmas is _____ December 25th. But what about Video Game Day? It's _____ September 12th. And Thank You Day? It's _____ September 18th. Here are some good holidays for the family: Sisters' Day is _____ August 4th, Aunts' and Uncles' Day is _____ July 16th, and Family Week is _____ May. But my favorite holiday is _____ September. It's _____ September 4th – that's Teacher's Day!

3 Complete the sentences with *in* or *on* and your own information.

    1. My first day of school is _____ .

    2. My birthday is _____ .

    3. I'm always happy _____ .

    4. There are a lot of holidays _____ .

Connections

1 Look at the information. Match the questions to the correct answers.

Name Paul Lee
Country Pusan, South Korea
Birthday April 12
Favorite holiday Korean Thanksgiving, August

Name Isabel Santos
Country Buenos Aires, Argentina
Birthday August 14
Favorite holiday New Year's Day, January

1. Is Paul from Japan? •

2. What is Paul's favorite holiday? •

3. When is Isabel's birthday? •

4. Is Isabel Colombian? •

5. When is Paul's birthday? •

6. What is Isabel's favorite holiday? •

7. What is Paul's last name? •

8. When is New Year's Day? •

• It's on August 14th.

• It's New Year's Day.

• No, he isn't. He's from South Korea.

• No, she isn't. She's Argentinian.

• It's Korean Thanksgiving.

• It's on April 12th.

• It's in January.

• It's Lee.

2 Answer the questions with short answers.

1. Is Paul from Venezuela? _No, he isn't._

2. Is Isabel from Buenos Aires? _____

3. Are Paul and Isabel from North America? _____

4. Is Pusan in South Korea? _____

5. Is Paul's favorite holiday in August? _____

6. Is Isabel's birthday in June? _____

7. Are Paul and Isabel Indian? _____

8. Is Isabel's favorite holiday in July? _____

36 Favorite places

1 Circle the correct words to complete the sentences.

1. My favorite store is Hip-Hop Clothes. There are cool clothes in the store and it's always (crowded / quiet).

2. There are a lot of museums, parks, and restaurants in London.
   It's (cute / exciting). It isn't (boring / happy).

3. The beach is my favorite place for a vacation. There aren't a lot of stores at the beach, and it's (beautiful / noisy).

4. The city zoo has lots of animals. It's (fun / old), and the animals are cute.

5. The Getty Museum in Los Angeles isn't (boring / crazy). You can learn a lot there. It's very (small / interesting).

2 Complete the conversation with the sentences in the box.

☐ It's really interesting.	☐ What's your favorite place in Florida, Steve?
☐ It's the Kennedy Space Center.	☑ What's your favorite place in Florida, Talisa?
☐ What's it like?	

Steve _What's your favorite place in Florida, Talisa?_

Talisa It's Disney World.

Steve _____

Talisa It's exciting. There are a lot of fun things there. There are cartoon characters, stores, and restaurants.

Steve Wow! That's great.

Talisa _____

Steve _____

Talisa What's it like?

Steve _____

Talent show

1 Unscramble and write the words.

1. l y a p   i g n P – g o n P   *play Ping-Pong*
2. s n i g _____
3. k r a a b d e t s o _____
4. w r a d _____
5. c a n d e _____
6. y l a p   e h t   t r a i u g _____

2 Number the sentences in the correct order.

_____ Great! I can sing. Let's enter.

_____ Can Mary sing?

_____ No. I can't dance at all. But I can play the guitar.

_____ You and me? Good idea!

_1_ It's a talent show. Hey! There's Mary's name.

_____ No, she can't. But she can dance.

_____ Can you dance?

3 Look at the pictures. Write questions and answers.

1

Q: *Can he sing?*

A: *No, he can't.*

2

Q: _____

A: _____

3

Q: _____

A: _____

4

Q: _____

A: _____

4 Write sentences about yourself. Use *I can* and *I can't*.

1. _____
2. _____
3. _____
4. _____
5. _____
6. _____

1 Answer the questions with the information in the chart.

	Jorge	Cara
sing	☐	☑
draw	☑	☑
play the guitar	☑	☐
dance	☐	☑

1. Can Cara play the guitar? *No, she can't.*

2. Can Jorge draw? _____

3. Can Cara dance? _____

4. Can Jorge sing? _____

5. Can Cara draw? _____

6. Can Jorge dance? _____

2 Unscramble the questions. Then answer the questions with your own information.

1. class / English / like / What's

   What's English class like?

   _____

2. friend / skateboard / Can / your / best ?

   _____

   _____

3. read / you / Spanish / Can ?

   _____

   _____

4. your / What's / math / like / class ?

   _____

   _____

5. favorite / city / What's / like / your ?

   _____

   _____

6. guitar / English / your / Can / play / teacher / th◗

   _____

   _____

3 Complete conversation 1. Then complete conversation 2 with your own information.

1. **A** What's your favorite place in Puerto Rico?

   B *It's Old San Juan.* (Old San Juan)

   A What's it like?

   B _____ (beautiful / interesting)

2. **A** _____ in your town?

   B _____

   A What's it like?

   B _____

38 School fashion

1 Label the clothes with the words in the box.

1 blouse		pants		shoes		skirt		socks	tie
jacket		shirt		shorts		sneakers		sweater	T-shirt

TARA   TAKESHI   MARK

2 Write questions.

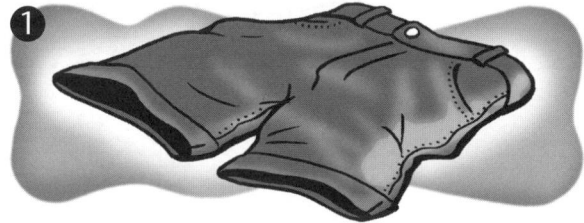

What color are the shorts?

They're blue.

They're green and white.

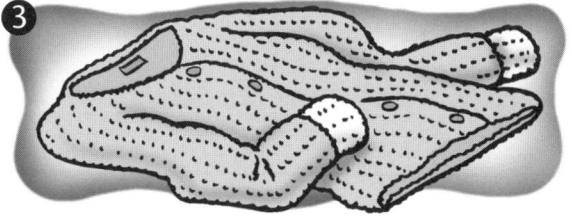

It's green.

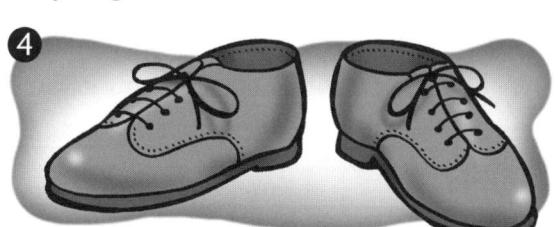

They're brown.

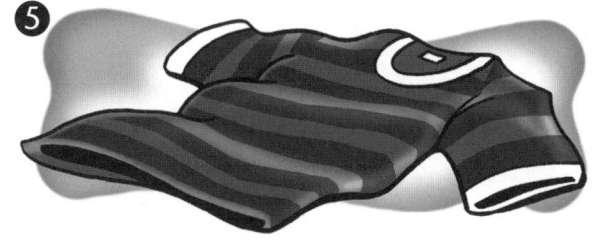

It's blue and red.

It's pink and purple.

Teen tastes

1 Write each conversation in the correct order.

1. ☐ Oh, I don't like rap music. I like pop music.

   ☐ It's my new rap CD. My favorite music is rap.

   ☑ What's this?

   A *What's this?*

   B _____

   A _____

2. ☐ I like pop music, too. But my favorite music is classical.

   ☐ I like pop music. What about you, Amy?

   ☐ That's great! I like classical music, too.

   A _____

   B _____

   A _____

2 Are these statements true or false for you? Check (✓) True or False.
Then correct the false statements.

	True	False
1. I don't like comic books. I think they're boring.	☐	☑
I love comic books. They're cool.		
2. I love classical music. It's beautiful.	☐	☐
3. I don't like basketball. I think it's difficult.	☐	☐
4. I like science. It's easy for me.	☐	☐
5. I don't like music stores. They're too noisy!	☐	☐

Lesson 40 Connections

1 Check (✓) the word that is different. Then write one more correct word.

1. ☐ draw   ☐ sing   ☑ picnic   ☐ play   <u>*dance*</u>

2. ☐ math   ☐ eraser   ☐ science   ☐ history   _____

3. ☐ pink   ☐ yellow   ☐ brown   ☐ easy   _____

4. ☐ radio   ☐ beach   ☐ zoo   ☐ museum   _____

5. ☐ shirt   ☐ blouse   ☐ shoes   ☐ dresser   _____

6. ☐ exciting   ☐ scary   ☐ park   ☐ interesting   _____

7. ☐ tennis   ☐ rock   ☐ rap   ☐ pop   _____

2 Complete the conversations with the questions in the box.

☐ Can you play tennis?
☐ Can your parents speak English?
☐ What color are your new socks?
☐ What color is your umbrella?
☐ What's the park like?
☑ What's your favorite sport?

1. **A** <u>*What's your favorite sport?*</u>

   B It's basketball. It's fun.

2. **A** _____

   B Yes, I can. I love playing tennis.

3. **A** _____

   B It's black and yellow. It's really cool.

4. **A** _____

   B No, they can't. But they can speak Spanish.

5. **A** _____

   B It's great. It has a small zoo.

6. **A** _____

   B They're green. My shoes are green, too!

Check Yourself - Unit 1

A Complete the conversation.

Janet Hi! ____ name is Janet. What's ____ name?

Sandy ____ Sandy. Nice to meet ____ .

B Label the pictures with the sentences in the box.

☐ Good afternoon.   ☐ Good evening.   ☐ Good morning.   ☐ Good night.

1. _____

2. _____

3. _____

4. _____

C Unscramble the sentences. Then match the sentences to the correct responses.

1. you / are / How / today ?

   _____

2. spell / do / How / name / you / your ?

   _____

3. to / Nice / you / meet .

   _____

4. Mrs. / afternoon, / Chu / Good .

   _____

5. later, / Simon / you / See .

   _____

6. name / is / Grace / My

   _____

a. B-R-Y-A-N.

b. Hi, Jasmine.

c. Good-bye, Pete.

d. Hi. My name is Diego.

e. Fine, thanks. How about you?

f. Nice to meet you, too.

Check Yourself - Unit 2

A Label the pictures with the words in the box.

☐ actor ☐ best friend ☐ model ☑ soccer coach
☐ basketball player ☐ cartoon character ☐ singer ☐ teacher

1. _soccer coach_ 2. _____ 3. _____ 4. _____

5. _____ 6. _____ 7. _____ 8. _____

B Write questions.

1. **Q:** _____
   A: I'm eleven.

2. **Q:** _____
   A: She's from Brazil.

3. **Q:** _____
   A: My name is Jeremy.

4. **Q:** _____
   A: He's my science teacher.

5. **Q:** _____
   A: His name is Charlie.

6. **Q:** _____
   A: She's not fifteen. She's seventeen.

C Choose the correct words to complete the paragraphs.

1. I'm Jack. This is my favorite _cartoon character_
(cartoon character / soccer player). _____ (His / Her)
name is Sakura, and _____ (she's / her) from Japan.
_____ (I'm / I'm not) from Japan. I'm from Australia.
_____ (My / I'm) eleven. Sakura's not eleven.
She's only _____ (ten / twelve).

2. I'm Jamie. This is my favorite tennis player.
_____ (He's / She's) from Brazil. _____ (Her / His)
name is Gustavo Kuerten. _____ (I'm / He's) from the U.S
_____ (I'm not / I'm) from Canada.

Check Yourself - Unit 3

A **Complete the sentences. Use *a*, *an*, or *the*.**

1. What's this? It's ___*a*___ cell phone.
2. That's _____ electronic organizer.
3. My books are on _____ computer.
4. It's _____ alarm clock. It's weird.
5. Jim's bag is next to _____ chair.
6. **A** What's that? _____ video game?

   B No, it isn't. It's _____ calculator.

B **Look at the picture. Whose things are these? Write Jay's sentences. Begin with *That's*, *This is*, *These are*, or *Those are*.**

(watch)   *This is my watch.*

(pens)   *Those are Cara's pens.*

1. (bicycle) _____
2. (pencil case) _____
3. (backpack) _____
4. (comic books) _____
5. (erasers) _____
6. (notebook) _____
7. (hat) _____
8. (pencils) _____
9. (cell phone) _____

C **Complete the conversation with the words in the box.**

☐ in   ☐ next to   ☐ on   ☐ under   ☑ Where are   ☐ where's

Leo ___*Where are*___ my books?

Mrs. Rivera They're _____ your bag.

Leo OK, but _____ my bag?

Mrs. Rivera It's _____ your desk.

Leo Where is my camera?

Mrs. Rivera It's _____ your desk.

Leo Thanks. Oh! Where's my basketball?

Mrs. Rivera It's _____ your chair, Leo!

Check Yourself - Unit 4

A Look at the map. Answer the questions with *Yes, it is* or *No, it's not.*

1. Is the restaurant on Elm Street?

   _____

2. Is the parking lot behind the
   movie theater?

   _____

3. Is the shoe store next to the café?

   _____

4. Is the bank across from the drugstore?

   _____

5. Is the bus stop in front of the bank?

   _____

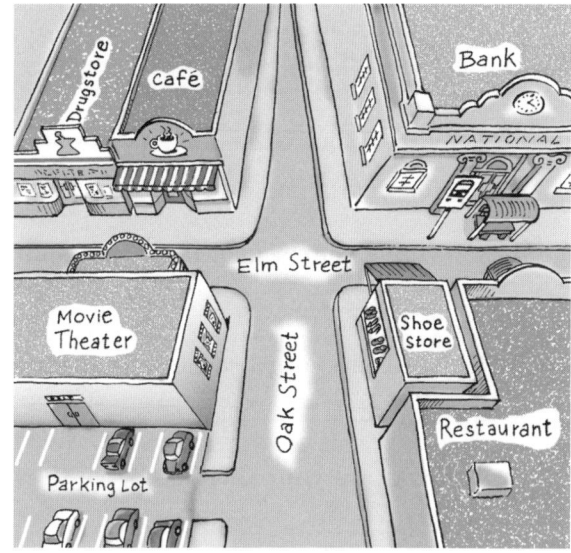

B Complete the questions with *Are* or *Is*. Then match the questions to
the answers.

1. *Are* you at home? _*d*_   a. No, they aren't. They're late.
2. ____ the park near the school? ____   b. No, it's not. It's on State Street.
3. ____ Ben and Jill here? ____   c. No, he's not. He's at the movie theater.
4. ____ you hot? ____   d. Yes, I am. I'm in my bedroom.
5. ____ the bank on Main Street? ____ e. Yes, I am. Let's go swimming.
6. ____ James at home? ____   f. Yes, it is. It's next to the school.

C Complete the conversations with the sentences in the box.

> ☑ I'm bored.   ☐ I'm hot.   ☐ I'm hungry.   ☐ I'm thirsty.   ☐ I'm tired.

1. **A** *I'm bored.* _____
   B Me, too. Let's play basketball.

2. **A** _____
   B Have a soda.

3. **A** _____
   B Let's sit down.

4. **A** _____
   B Have a sandwich.

5. **A** _____
   B Me, too. Let's go swimming.

Check Yourself - Unit 5

A Answer the questions. Use *it's, he's, she's, they're,* or *I'm* and the words in the box.

☐ big ☐ happy ☐ old ☐ quiet ☑ tall

1. **A** What's your aunt like? Is she short?

   B No, *she's not. She's tall.*

2. **A** What's your school like? Is it small?

   B No, _____

3. **A** What are your brothers like? Are they noisy?

   B No, _____

4. **A** What are your CDs like? Are they new?

   B No, _____

5. **A** Are you sad today?

   B No, _____

B Complete the paragraph with *we, our, they,* or *their.*

My family and our neighbors are different.
Our house is small, and _____ house is big.
_____ have a nice yard, and _____ have no yard.
But we like _____ house. _____ like their house, too.

C Complete the sentences. Use *has* or *has no.*

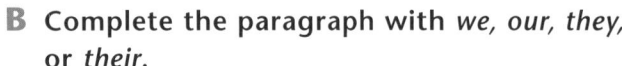

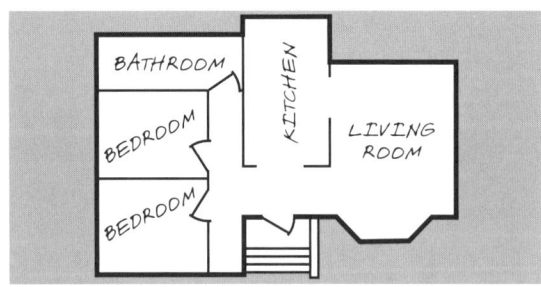

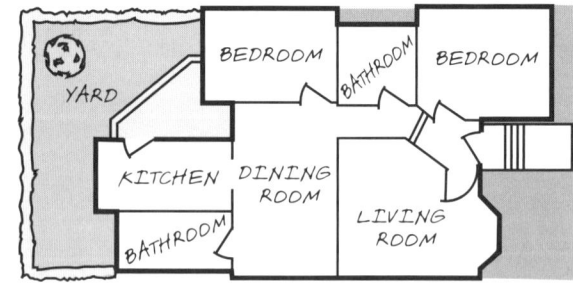

Jane's house

1. *It has two* _____ bedrooms.
2. _____ dining room.
3. _____ living room.

Tim's house

1. _____ yard.
2. _____ bathrooms.
3. _____ garage.

Check Yourself - Unit 6

A Look at the picture. Write questions and answers.

1. (CDs)   **Q:** _Are there any CDs?_   **A:** _Yes, there are._

2. (CD player)   **Q:** _____   **A:** _____

3. (computers)   **Q:** _____   **A:** _____

4. (printers)   **Q:** _____   **A:** _____

5. (VCR)   **Q:** _____   **A:** _____

6. (bookcase)   **Q:** _____   **A:** _____

B Look at the picture. Write sentences with *There's a, There's no, There are,* or *There are no.*

1. (bookcase)   _There's no bookcase._

2. (cabinets)   _____

3. (screen)   _____

4. (books)   _____

5. (chairs)   _____

6. (CD player)   _____

C Write sentences about Gary's schedule.

1. _His English class is at 1:30._

2. _____

3. _____

4. _____

5. _____

6. _____

GARY'S SCHEDULE

Event
1. English class 1:30
2. history class 8:15
3. music class Friday
4. health class Wednesday
5. geography class 10:35
6. science class 10:45

Check Yourself - Unit 7

A Complete the conversation with *is, isn't, are,* or *aren't*.

Kim Hi, Mia. _Are_ those your CDs?

Mia Yes, they _____ . This _____ Luciana Mello. She's my favorite singer.

Kim _____ she famous?

Mia No, she _____ . But she's great.

Kim _____ all your favorite singers Brazilian?

Mia No, they _____ . I like American singers, too.

B Write questions.

1. **A** (England)   _Is he from England?_ _____
   B Yes, he is. He's British.

2. **A** (Peruvian) _____
   B No, they aren't. Tia and Marie are Colombian.

3. **A** (April) _____
   B No, it isn't. Mother's Day is in May.

4. **A** (good) _____
   B Yes, they are. The Orioles are a great baseball team!

5. **A** (Brazil) _____
   B No, he isn't. He's from Puerto Rico.

C Write sentences about people's birthdays.

	Month	Day
1. Sebastian	9	5
2. Shannon	2	21
3. Mr. Brock	12	
4. Paco	4	11
5. Kelly	8	

1. _Sebastian's birthday is on September 5th._
2. _____
3. _____
4. _____
5. _____

D Write the words.

1. 14th _fourteenth_ _____
2. 4th _____
3. 23rd _____
4. 9th _____
5. 16th _____
6. 22nd _____

Check Yourself - Unit 8

A Complete the conversations with the questions in the box.

> ☐ What color are your shoes?   ☐ What is the zoo like?
> ☐ What color is your cell phone? ☑ What's your school like?

1. **A** _What's your school like?_
   B It's crowded. It has a lot of students.

2. **A** _____
   B It's pink. It's really cute!

3. **A** _____
   B It's interesting. There are a lot of animals.

4. **A** _____
   B They're blue. They're old, too.

B Match the questions to the answers.

1. What's your favorite food?	_e_	a. Rap. It's really cool!
2. What's your favorite school subject?	___	b. She's nice. And she can play very well!
3. What's your math class like?	___	c. It's boring. I don't like math.
4. What's the museum like?	___	d. I like science. It's fun.
5. What's your favorite music?	___	e. Italian. I love pizza!
6. What's your soccer coach like?	___	f. It's crowded, but very interesting.

C Complete the paragraph with *can, can't, like, love,* or *don't like.*

My favorite place in Sydney is Bondi Beach. It's very exciting and interesting.
I _don't like_ boring places. I _____ the water and the sun. I _____ swim
very well, too. My brother _____ swim. But he _____ skateboard! So Bondi
Beach is his favorite place, too.

Illustration Credits

Michael Brennan 6, 15, 18 *(top)*, 20, 30, 55
Andrea Champlin 14, 21, 32, 52
Laurie Conley 7, 13, 18 *(bottom)*, 19 (top), 27, 48
David Coulson 11, 17, 23, 25, 52
Bruce Day 2, 24, 31, 38, 42, 53 *(bottom)*
Adam Hurwitz 35, 54 *(bottom)*
Larry Jones 3, 19 *(bottom)*, 26, 34, 45, 47, 50, 54 *(top)*
Andrew Schiff 5, 8, 16, 22, 28, 53 *(top)*, 56

Photographic Credits

2 ©Corbis

3 ©Getty Images

4 *(top)* ©Getty Images; *(bottom)* ©Corbis

7 ©Getty Images

9 *(top to bottom)* ©AFP/Corbis; ©Frank Trapper/Corbis; ©Duomo/Corbis; ©Reuters/Corbis; ©Gregory Pace/Corbis; ©Courtesy of United Media; 10 (clockwise from top left) ©Getty Images; ©Getty Images; ©Reuters/Corbis; ©Getty Images

12 ©Michael Newman/Photo Edit

13 *(left)* ©Reuters/Corbis; *(right)* ©Rufus F. Folkks/Corbis

15 ©SW Production/Index Stock

17 *(bottom left)* ©Getty Images

20 ©Getty Images

24 ©Getty Images

29 *(top group clockwise from top left)* ©Getty Images; ©Stanley Rowin/Index Stock; ©Getty Images; ©Digital Vision; ©Getty Images

29 *(center)* ©Richard Berenholz/Corbis; *(bottom)* ©Getty Images

32 *(top row)* ©Hemera; ©Getty Images; ©Hemera; ©Getty Images

32 *(side row, top to bottom)* ©Superstock; ©Getty Images; ©Corbis; ©Getty Images

33 *(top)* ©David Schmidt/Master File; *(bottom)* ©Getty Images

34 ©Patrick Bennett/Corbis

35 ©Getty Images

37 ©Getty Images

39 ©Getty Images

40 *(top)* ©Sygma Corbis; *(bottom)* ©Simonpietri Christian/Corbis Sygma

41 ©Piotr Powietrzynski/Picture Quest

43 *(top)* ©Getty Images; *(bottom)* ©HIRB/Index Stock

44 *(left)* ©Jonathan Blair/Corbis; *(right)* (©Museum of Flight/Corbis

46 *(top left)* ©Tom and Dee Ann McCarthy/Corbis; *(top right)* ©Corbis; *(bottom)* ©Getty Images

49 *(top)* ©Getty Images; *(bottom)* ©Jonathan Blair/Corbis ©Jim Cummins/Corbis

51 *(clockwise from top left)* Rafael Roa/Corbis; ©Reuters/Corbis; ©Reuters/Corbis; ©Getty Images; ©Mitchell Gerber/Corbis; © Getty Images; ©Reuters/Corbis; *(bottom of page)* ©Reuters/Corbis

56 ©Craig Witkowski/Index Stock

57 *(top)* ©Getty Images; *(bottom right)* ©Dave G. Houser/Corbis; ©Paul A. Souders/Corbis

Notes

Notes

Notes

Notes